PA-28 Cherokee
A Pilot's Guide

Jeremy M. Pratt

Aviation Supplies & Academics, Inc.
Newcastle, Washington

U.S. Edition 1995

© 1995 Aviation Supplies & Academics, Inc.

First published in England by Airplan Flight Equipment, Ltd.
and Jeremy M. Pratt, 1992

PA-28 Cherokee: A Pilot's Guide
Jeremy M. Pratt

ASA-PG-PA-28C
ISBN 1-56027-215-5

Aviation Supplies & Academics, Inc.
Newcastle, Washington

Printed in the United States of America

02 01 00 99   9 8 7 6 5 4 3 2

Library of Congress Cataloging-in-Publication Data:

Pratt, Jeremy M.
    PA-28 Cherokee / Jeremy M. Pratt. — U.S. ed.
        p.   cm.   — (A pilot's guide)
    Includes index.
    ISBN 1-56027-215-5
    1. Piper PA-28 (Private planes) I. Title. II. Series: Pratt, Jeremy M. Pilot's guide.
TL686.P5P73 1995
629.132'5217—dc20
                                          95-15210
                                             CIP

Acknowledgements

I would like to thank all those whose knowledge, help and advice went into this book; in particular:

Airspeed Aviation
Air Nova
Simon Booth
CAA Safety Promotion Section
CSE Aviation
Colourmatch
Adrian Dickinson
Steve Dickinson
David Hockings
Andy Holland
Phil Huntington

Wendy Mellor
Manchester School of Flying
Margaret Parkes
Paul Price
Ravenair
Neil Rigby
John Ross
Ian Sixsmith
John Thorpe
Visual Eyes

Sarah, Kate and Miles

Jeremy M. Pratt
August 1992

Contents

Section 3 – Handling the Piper PA28 Cherokee

Section 4 – Mixture and Carburetor Icing Supplement

Section 5 – Expanded PA-28 Pre-Flight Check List

Section 6 – Loading and Performance

Section 7 – Conversions

Index

Editor's Note

Welcome to ASA's *A Pilot's Guide* series by Jeremy Pratt. In this guide, you'll learn from the experts the general principles involved in flying the PA-28 Cherokee, with extra insight on individual characteristics gleaned from flying experience.

PA-28 Cherokee: A Pilot's Guide is not an authoritative document. Material in this book is presented for the purposes of orientation, familiarization, and comparison only.

Performance figures are based upon the indicated weights, standard atmospheric conditions, level hard-surface dry runways, and no wind. They are values based upon calculations derived from flight tests conducted by the aircraft company under carefully documented conditions and using professional test pilots. Performance will vary with individual aircraft and numerous other factors affecting flight.

The approved *Pilot's Operating Handbook* and/or the approved *Airplane Flight Manual* is the only source of authoritative information for any individual aircraft. In the interests of safety and good airmanship, the pilot should be familiar with these documents.

Section 1
General Description

Introduction to the PA-28 Cherokee

Cherokee—a Native-American tribe that dwelled in the North Carolina and Tennessee area.

The PA-28 Cherokee, first produced in 1961, continued the Piper penchant for using Native-American tribal names for their aircraft. The Cherokee was introduced to replace the high wing, fabric covered PA-22 Tri-Pacer, and also to compete with the hugely successful Cessna singles that had been introduced a few years previously.

Even the early Cherokees were available in many forms and different options. These versions and derivatives continued to spawn down the years giving a whole array of Cherokees in existence, from the fixed gear, two-place 140 HP through 150 HP, 160 HP, 180 HP and 235 HP models, to the PA-32 Cherokee Six and retractable Arrows. If you continue to follow the lineage through the Warrior models with their re-designed wing, and the Lance and Saratoga (derivatives of the original PA-32 Cherokee Six), you end up with far too many types to cover in the scope of this book. Production of the fixed gear Cherokees amounts to around 25,000 aircraft; if you include all the various derivatives you come to a figure nearer 43,000.

This publication will cover the Cherokee in its fixed gear models powered by the 150 HP and 180 HP engines, (although much of the information in this book will be relevant to the 140 HP, 160 HP and 235 HP models), from 1963 to the introduction of the new style wing beginning in 1974. The later models, still with the PA-28 designation but renamed the Warrior, are the subject of a separate publication in this series. It is generally good airmanship, but particularly with the prolific PA-28 variants, to remember that the individual airplane flight manual (as amended and updated) is the only authoritative document for the particular aircraft you intend to fly.

MODEL YEAR	MODEL	PRODUCTION NAME
1964 – 1968	PA-28-140	Cherokee 140
1969	PA-28-140	Cherokee 140 B
1970	PA-28-140	Cherokee 140 C
1971	PA-28-140	Cherokee 140 D †
1972	PA-28-140	Cherokee 140 E * †
1973 – 1977	PA-28-140	Cherokee 140 * †

Key to Symbols

* also known as the Cruiser
† two seat variant known as the Flite Liner

MODEL YEAR	MODEL	PRODUCTION NAME
1963 – 1964	PA-28-180	Cherokee 180 B
1965 – 1967	PA-28-180	Cherokee 180 C
1968 – 1969	PA-28-180	Cherokee 180 D

MODEL YEAR	MODEL	PRODUCTION NAME
1973 – 1974	PA-28-180	Challenger
1974 – 1975	PA-28-180	Archer

The Airframe

The PA-28 airframe is generally described as being of all metal construction. The primary structure is constructed of aluminum alloy, and the engine mount is made from tubular steel. Some non-structural components such as the wing tips and landing gear fairings are made from fiberglass.

The fuselage has a semi-monocoque structure; that is, the vertical bulkheads and frames are joined by horizontal longerons and stringers which run the length of the fuselage. The metal skin is riveted to the longerons and stringers. This arrangement is conventional for modern light aircraft and allows loads to be spread over the whole construction. At the rear of the fuselage the tail unit incorporates an "all-moving" horizontal stabilizer, or stabilator. Underneath the rear fuselage a triangular combined tie-down point and tail guard is fitted.

The wings are of cantilever design (unsupported by external struts or bracing), and have a positive dihedral. On the upper surface of the right wing, a black walkway is marked; this is the only area of the wing to be walked on or stood on. Underneath each wing a metal ring is fitted to be used as a tie-down point.

The wings have a positive dihedral.

The Flight Controls

Dual flight controls are installed as standard and link the cockpit controls to the control surfaces via cable linkages.

The AILERONS are of the differential type, moving upward through 30°, and downward through 15°. A balance weight is installed on a short rod at the outer end of each aileron, and this weight is visible inside the wing tip cavity.

The FLAPS are of the simple slotted type. They are manually operated from a lever between the cockpit seats, through a torque tube and push rods to the flap surfaces. Four positions can be selected, fully up (0°), 10°, 25° and 40°. The flaps lock in the full up position, and only in this position can the walkway on the right hand flap be stood upon. In any other position, the flaps will move rapidly down to 40° if any weight is placed on the flap walkway, dumping the unwary onto the ground!

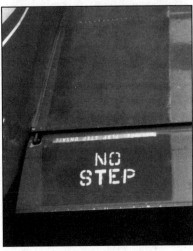

Flap "No Step" warning.

The RUDDER is operated from the rudder pedals (which are also linked to the steerable nose wheel) and can move through 27° either side of the neutral position. A rudder trim tab is fitted in the cockpit below the instrument panel. This wheel can be used to trim out excessive rudder forces in flight. As the rudder is connected (via rods from the rudder pedals) to the nose wheel, the control surface cannot be moved while the aircraft is stationary without exerting considerable force—and this is not recommended.

The Cherokee has an all moving STABILATOR, which functions as a combined horizontal stabilizer and elevator, it moves up 14° from neutral and down 2° from neutral. The control functions in the natural sense, and by design provides a very powerful pitching force.

The Cherokee tail section.

As part of its design the stabilator incorporates an ANTI-BALANCE TAB at its trailing edge, sometimes referred to as an anti-servo tab. This tab combines two functions. It moves in the same direction as the stabilator to provide a "damping" force, increasing the feel of the control, which is very important with such a powerful control surface. In addition, the anti-balance tab acts as a trim tab to trim out pitch forces on the control wheel; the control surface moves 3° up from neutral and 12° down from neutral. Depending on the year of construction, the cockpit control for the anti-balance tab is either a roof-mounted handle that rotates clockwise and counter-clockwise, or a conventional trim wheel located on the cockpit floor between the seats. The floor-mounted trim wheel acts in the normal sense, rotating the wheel forward to trim nose down and backward to trim nose up.

Roof-mounted trim handle.

Floor-mounted trim wheel.

The Landing Gear

The Cherokee LANDING GEAR is fixed and is a tricycle-type, with a nose wheel.

The main landing gear incorporates an air/oil oleo strut to absorb operating loads; normally the main gear struts should have about 4.5 inches of the piston tube exposed. The main landing gear is fitted with 6.00 X 6 wheels, and may have optional wheel fairings. The nose gear attaches to the engine mount and also has an air/oil oleo strut to damp and absorb the normal operating loads, normally about 3.25 inches of the piston tube should be exposed. On the rear of the nose leg a torque link is installed to maintain the correct alignment of the nose wheel; its lower arm is fitted to the nose wheel fork and the upper arm to the oleo cylinder casing. The nose gear is steerable through direct linkage to the rudder pedals. A spring device aids nose wheel and rudder centering, and is also adjustable to act as the rudder trim (*see* "Rudder," page 1-7). From 1974 models on, bungee springs are incorporated on the push rods to aid lighter and smoother nose wheel steering; without these bungees the nose wheel steering can be rather heavy. The nose wheel tire is a 6.00 X 6 unit. In common with just about all light aircraft, the nose gear is not as strong as the main gear.

Main landing gear with optional spats.

Nose wheel assemble with optional spats.

The tire grooves should have at least 1/16 inch depth over 75% of the tire to be serviceable. Additionally, if the tread across the width of the tire is worn to less than 1/16 inch in any one place, the tire will need replacing.

Hand brake lever.   *The brake fluid reservoir.*

The BRAKE system consists of single disc brake assemblies fitted to the main landing gear and operated by a hydraulic system. The brake lever in the cockpit operates a master cylinder located below and behind the control panel. When the control is pulled back, braking is evenly applied to both main wheels. A small button on the right of the brake lever allows it to be locked in the ON position, to act as a parking brake. To release the parking brake, the control is pulled back (which unlatches the button), and then pushed fully forward. When optional toe brakes are installed, they are operated by depressing the upper half of the rudder pedal. With this system each toe brake has a separate brake cylinder above the pedal, and it is possible to operate the brakes differentially—to the left or right wheel. This system allows the aircraft to turn in a very tight circle, and it is possible to lock one main wheel with the use of some pedal force. Turning around a wheel in this fashion tends to "scrub" the tire, and is generally discouraged. A brake fluid reservoir is fitted to the upper left forward face of the firewall (accessed via the left engine cowling). Here it can be inspected for fluid level and replenished if necessary.

The Engine

The Cherokee 140 is fitted with a Lycoming 0-320-E engine of 150 HP at 2,700 RPM (some very early models were fitted with a 140 HP unit). The Cherokee 180 has a Lycoming 0-360-A engine of 180 HP at 2,700 RPM. The 320 and 360 designators refer to the cubic capacity of the engine in inches. Apart from this difference, the two engines are similar and are treated as one subject, below.

The engine is a four cylinder unit, with cylinders horizontally opposed across the crankshaft. The cylinders are staggered so that each connecting rod has its own crankshaft throw. The cylinders and crankcase assembly are fashioned from aluminum alloy castings.

The engine is air-cooled. Airflow enters the engine compartment at the front of the cowling, and is directed by baffles to flow over the whole engine. The cylinders feature deep cooling fins to aid cooling. The airflow leaves the engine compartment at the rear lower cowling underneath the engine compartment. The engine is mounted on a steel tubular mounting which attaches to the firewall.

Port side view Lycoming 0-360-A engine (with cowling removed).

The Propeller

The PROPELLER is an all-metal, two-bladed, fixed pitch design, turned by direct drive from the engine crankshaft. It rotates clockwise as seen from the cockpit. For the Cherokee 140, the diameter is 74", with a minimum allowable diameter of 72.5". The Cherokee 180 propeller has a diameter of 76".

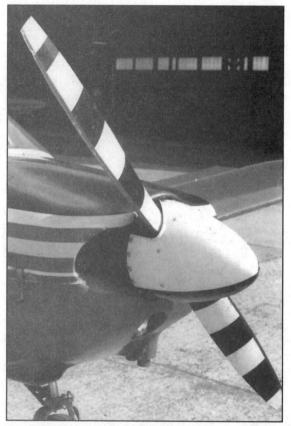

PA-28-180 propeller, painted black and white to be more visible.

The Ignition System

The engine features a dual ignition system, fitted with two magnetos. The magnetos are small AC generators which are driven by the crankshaft rotation to provide a very high voltage to a distributor, which directs it via high voltage leads (or high tension leads) to the spark plugs. At the spark plug the current must cross a gap; in doing so a spark is produced which ignites the fuel/air mixture in the cylinder.

The magnetos are fitted at the rear of the engine, one each side of the engine center line (hence, Left and Right magnetos). The usual arrangement is for each magneto to fire the bottom spark plugs of the two cylinders on one side of the engine, and the top spark plugs on the other side. Each cylinder has two spark plugs (top and bottom) for safety and efficiency. The leads that run from the magnetos to the spark plugs should be secure, and there should be no splits or cracks in the plastic insulation covering the leads.

It is worth emphasizing that the ignition system is totally independent of the aircraft electrical system, and once the engine is running it will operate regardless of the serviceability of the battery or alternator.

The Oil System

The engine's oil system provides lubrication, cooling, sealing, cleansing and protection against corrosion. The system is a wet-sump, pressure feed system. The oil sump is located under the engine, and oil is drawn from here by the engine-driven oil pump, through a cooler and filter and into the oil gallery of the right half of the crankcase. When the oil has flowed

PA-28-180 oil filler door in the top of the engine cowling.

around the engine it drains down to the sump by gravity. An oil pressure relief valve is fitted in the upper right side of the crankcase. The function of this valve is to maintain the correct operating pressure over a wide range of temperatures and RPM settings. Above a certain pressure, the valve will open and allow oil to return to the sump rather than continuing into the lubricating system.

Oil quantity can be checked on a dipstick on the right side of the engine. The dipstick is graduated in U.S. quarts and measures the quantity of the oil in the sump. When the engine has been running, the oil will take up to 10 minutes to return to the sump; only then can a true reading be taken. When replacing the dipstick, care should be taken not to overtighten the cap. To do so may make it exceptionally difficult to open the cap again, and it is possible to strip the thread on the cap or filler tube.

The oil temperature gauge and oil pressure gauge in the cockpit enable the pilot to monitor the health of the oil system.

Later model Cherokees (1975 on) are fitted with an annunciator panel at the top center of the instrument panel below the compass. This panel has three warning lights for VAC (vacuum), OIL (oil pressure) and ALT (electrical system). A test button is fitted to check the operation of the lights when the engine is running. The OIL warning light illuminates if oil pressure falls below 35 psi.

Oil filler pipe.

The Starter System

The starter motor is housed at the lower front left side of the engine. It incorporates a geared cog that engages with the teeth of the starter ring when the starter is operated. As the engine is turned, an impulse coupling in the left magneto operates; this retards the spark and aids starting. When the engine fires and begins to rotate under its own power, this impulse coupling ceases to operate and normal spark timing is resumed. When the key is released, allowing it to return to the BOTH position, the cog on the starter motor withdraws to be clear of the starter ring.

Starter ring, located behind the propeller.

The Fuel System

The Cherokee has two aluminum fuel tanks, located in the inboard leading edge of each wing. From these tanks, a fuel line runs through the wing and fuselage to the fuel selector valve located on the left lower cockpit wall in the pilot footwell. From this valve, the fuel line runs through the firewall to a fuel strainer bowl mounted on the forward left face of the firewall. From the strainer bowl, a fuel line runs through the electric fuel pump and engine-driven fuel pump to the carburetor. A separate line runs from the strainer bowl to the cockpit primer, and from there to the inlet manifold.

Underwing fuel tank vent.

Each tank has a TANK VENT, which is a forward facing pipe on the lower surface of the wing. It ensures that ambient pressure is maintained above the fuel in the fuel tank. Should this vent become blocked, a vacuum may form in the tank as the fuel level lowers, and fuel flow to the engine may be interrupted.

There are three FUEL STRAINERS, one at the lower rear inboard edge of each tank, accessible from the inboard lower wing surface, and one from the fuel bowl, accessed at the lower left cowling. Fuel can only be drawn from the bowl if the cockpit fuel selector is in the Left or Right position. The shape of the fuel strainers has been the cause of problems. To take a fuel sample the bar of the strainer is pushed up against a spring, and fuel will flow into the fuel tester. When the bar is released, it should return to its original position, and the fuel flow ceases. The original strainer has a "lip," which makes it possible for the valve to lock in the open position, and fuel to continue to drain through the valve even after the bar has been released. If this occurs to the tank strainers, the result will be the loss of fuel from the tanks, and possible fuel exhaustion.

If the engine fuel strainer is open, the likely result is engine failure just after takeoff due to fuel starvation. In documented incidents, the fuel was *not* turned on for the fuel drain check, and so the fact that the engine fuel strainer was locked open was missed. The start, taxi, power checks and takeoff were normal; however, the engine failed just after takeoff.

A recommended modification is to file off an area of the strainer valve so that the bar cannot lock in the open position. Exercise care when operating the fuel drains, wherever this modification has not been carried out.

The cockpit FUEL SELECTOR of the Cherokee can also be a problem. The selector is located on the lower left cockpit wall of the pilot's footwell, and so is not easily accessible to a pilot in the right seat (instructor, for example). Exercise particular care when moving the selector lever, since it is somewhat out of sight of the pilot. The selector can be used to feed the engine from either the Left or Right tank. To turn the fuel off, a spring loaded latch on the selector must first be depressed, and then the lever rotated to the OFF position. This operation can be a two-handed operation, which should help prevent the accidental selection of the off position; although it is apparently still possible to accidentally turn the fuel OFF while airborne.

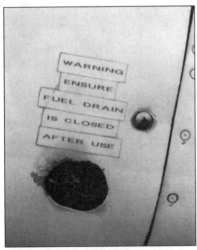

Engine fuel strainer with warning sign.

Cockpit fuel selector (left tank selected).

In normal operation, the fuel is drawn through the system by an engine-driven FUEL PUMP. Should this pump fail, however, the fuel supply to the carburetor will cease and the engine will stop. Therefore a second, electrical fuel pump is installed. This pump is selected ON or OFF from a cockpit switch. Normally, the electric fuel pump is used during takeoff and landing, and when changing tanks. A fuel pressure gauge is installed, reading from a sender between the engine driven fuel pump and the carburetor.

The Carburetor

The CARBURETOR mixes air with the fuel from the fuel system and supplies the fuel/air mix to the cylinders. The carburetor is located under the engine, and takes induction air from a scoop intake in the lower front cowling. This air is filtered and then fed into the carburetor air box. In this box, a butterfly valve is used to allow either the filtered air, or heated air, to be fed to the carburetor. Heated air comes from an unfiltered inlet tube which then passes into a shroud around the exhaust, which heats it before it reaches the carburetor. Hot or cold air is selected via the carburetor heat control in the cockpit; the use of this control and the subject of carburetor icing are fully discussed in Section 4. The fuel/air mix is carried from the carburetor to the induction manifold and to the inlet port of each cylinder.

Cockpit carburetor heat control.

The carburetor is fitted with an ACCELERATOR PUMP. With a standard carburetor, rapidly opening the throttle can lead to an excessively lean mixture, causing the engine to falter, often at an inconvenient moment. This is known as a "lean mixture out." The accelerator pump overcomes this problem by introducing a charge of fuel—if the throttle is opened quickly—to maintain the mixture. Unfortunately, the system is a little too effective on the Cherokees; opening the throttle too rapidly can actually lead to a "rich mixture out," caused by an overly rich mixture as the throttle is opened rapidly. Many Cherokees are fitted with a placard that warns the pilot not to go from idle to full throttle in less than 2 seconds.

The PRIMER control situated next to the throttle quadrant is an aid to starting. The control is unlocked by rotating the primer until a pin on the shaft aligns with the cut-out in the collar. The control can then be pulled out, filling the pump with fuel. The primer is then pushed in, delivering fuel to the primer nozzles. When priming is complete, the control should be pushed fully in with the pin aligned with the collar cut-out, and then rotated about half a turn. As a check, attempt to pull the primer out, it should remain locked. It is important that the primer is fully locked, otherwise engine rough-running may result.

The MIXTURE is controlled from the mixture lever located in the cockpit which adjusts the fuel/air ratio in the carburetor. The use of this control is covered in Section 4. In the full forward position, it gives a RICH mixture, and if moved to the rearward ICO (Idle Cut-Off) position, the fuel supply is cut off and the engine stops.

The power quadrant has a lever on the right side. Movement of this "friction" control adjusts the friction of the throttle and mixture levers, and allows for them to be kept in the desired position. Generally, this lever is adjusted to leave the throttle and mixture with relatively loose and easy movement on the ground, but is tightened to hold the levers in position for takeoff.

The Electrical System

The Cherokee has a 14 volt, direct current electrical system. The alternator is mounted to the front lower right of the engine and is engine driven from a belt drive off a pulley directly behind the starter ring. The alternator is rated at 60 amps (PA-28-140 models before 1969 and PA-28-180 models before 1966 have a 35 amp alternator). A 12 volt battery is located inside a vented box under the baggage compartment floor (PA-28-140), or aft of the baggage compartment (PA-28-180).

The ALTERNATOR is the primary source of power to the electrical system in normal operations with the engine running. The alternator produces alternating current (AC) which is converted into direct current (DC) by diodes incorporated in the alternator housing, which act as rectifiers. By their design, alternators require a small voltage (about 3 volts) to produce the electromagnetic field required inside the alternator. The significance of this is that if the battery is completely discharged (flat), the alternator will not be able to supply any power to the electrical system, even after the engine has been started by some other means (i.e., external power or hand propping). Output from the alternator is controlled by a VOLTAGE REGULATOR which is mounted behind the right-hand side of the instrument panel.

Electrical switch panel, the master switch is on the left hand side.

The primary purposes of the BATTERY are to provide power for engine starting, the initial excitation of the alternator, and as a backup in the event of alternator failure. In normal operations with the engine running, the alternator provides the power to the electrical system and charges the battery. A fully-charged battery has a charging rate of about 2 amperes. In a partially discharged condition (i.e., just after engine start) the charging rate can be much higher than this. In the event of an alternator failure, the battery provides *all* power to the electrical system. In theory a fully-charged 35-ampere-hour battery is capable of providing 35 amps for 1 hour, 1 amp for 35 hours, or 17.5 amps for 2 hours, etc. In practice, the power available is governed by factors such as battery age and condition, load placed on it, etc. The best advice is to reduce electrical load to the minimum consistent with safety, and plan to make a landing at the earliest opportunity, should an electrical failure occur.

The AMMETER indicates in amperes the electrical load on the alternator. With the engine running and all electrical services turned off, the ammeter will indicate the charging rate of the battery. As services are switched on, the ammeter will indicate the additional load of each item. For night flight, the maximum continuous load will be in the region of 30 amps. In the event of alternator failure the ammeter will indicate zero, and where installed a red "Low Voltage" warning light will illuminate. On later models (1975 and on) an annunciator panel is installed in the upper instrument panel (described in "The Oil System," page 1-14). The ALT warning light of the annunciator panel will illuminate if the alternator fails.

The pilot controls the electrical system via the MASTER SWITCH located on the left side of the instrument panel. This switch is a split rocker switch having two halves, labeled BAT and ALT. Normally the switch is operated as one, both halves being used together. The BAT half of the switch can be operated independently, so that all electrical power is being drawn from the battery only; however, the ALT side can only be turned on in conjunction with the BAT half. Should an electrical problem occur the MASTER Switch can be used to reset the electrical system by turning it OFF for 2 seconds, and then turning it ON again.

The aircraft may be fitted with an EXTERNAL POWER RECEPTACLE behind the wing root, this can be used to connect external power for starting or operation of the aircraft electrical system. Before using external power, it is imperative to check that the external power unit is of the correct voltage—otherwise *serious damage could be inflicted on the electrical system*. Additionally it should be remembered that if the battery is totally flat (completely discharged), it will need to be removed and recharged or replaced before flight.

To use external power the following procedure should be adopted:

1. Check that master switch and all electrical equipment are OFF.

2. Ensure that the *red* lead of the jumper cable goes to the *positive* terminal of the external power source and the *black* lead to the *negative*.

3. Insert the cable plug into the aircraft external power receptacle socket.

4. Turn the master switch ON, and proceed with normal starting procedure.

5. After engine start turn master switch and all electrical equipment OFF and remove the cable plug.

6. Turn the master switch ON, and check the ammeter. If no output is shown, flight should not be attempted.

The various electrically-operated systems are protected by individual CIRCUIT BREAKERS, which are located to the right side of the lower instrument panel. Should a problem occur (e.g., a short circuit), the relevant circuit breaker may "pop," and will be raised in relation to the other circuit breakers (CBs). The correct procedure is to allow the CB to cool for 2 minutes, then reset it and check the result. If the CB pops again it should not be reset.

External power receptacle.

Apart from engine starting and the alternator field, the electrical system supplies power to the following:

• All internal and external lights.

• All radios and intercom.

• Turn coordinator, Fuel gauges.

• Stall warning, Pitot heater, Electric fuel pump.

The Stall Warning System

A light located at the extreme left side of the instrument panel is electrically activated from a stall warning vane on the leading edge of the left wing. This vane moves up at angles of attack approaching the stall, and gives a warning at approximately 5 to 10 knots above the stall speed. The stall warning is inoperative with the master switch off, and may be inoperative with a faulty electrical system.

Cockpit stall warning light.

Wing mounted stall warning vane.

The Lighting System

The Cherokee may be equipped with a variety of optional internal and external lighting. Where wing tip "strobe" lights are installed, care should be used in their operation. As a general rule, the strobes are not used during taxiing, as they can dazzle and distract those nearby. They are, however, very effective in the air. If flying in cloud conditions or heavy precipitation, it is recommended that they be turned off, as

the pilot may become spatially disoriented. The landing light is fitted in the lower front nose cowling; again, it should be used with some discretion, because of the very short life of the light bulbs. Navigation lights are controlled from a thumb wheel in the electrical switch cluster, which also controls instrument panel lighting. When the switch is first turned on, the navigation lights are illuminated at their set brilliance. The wheel can be rotated to control the level of instrument panel lighting, but the navigation lights remain at their set brightness until the switch is turned fully off.

Light switches selected on, navigation lights thumb wheel far right.

The Vacuum System

An engine-driven vacuum pump is
mounted to the upper rear face of
the engine. This pump is fitted with
a plastic shear drive, so that
should the pump seize, the shear
drive will fail and the engine will not
be damaged. The air enters the
vacuum system through a filter,
passes through the air-driven gyro
instruments (and is measured by
the suction gauge), flows through a
vacuum regulator and into the

vacuum pump, from which it is expelled through a short pipe. On some
older models there may be no central filter; instead, paper filters are fitted
at the connection to each instrument.

Suction is used to drive the gyros in the attitude indicator (or artificial
horizon) and heading indicator (or direction indicator). A suction gauge
mounted on the instrument panel measures suction. For cruising RPMs
and altitudes, the reading should be 5.0, within 0.1 inches of mercury. At
1,200 RPM suction should be over 4.0; at higher or lower settings the
gyros may become unreliable. A lower suction reading over an extended
period may indicate a faulty vacuum regulator, dirty screens or a system
leak. If the vacuum pump fails or a line collapses, the suction gauge
reading will fall to zero; the attitude indicator and heading indicator will
become unreliable over a period of some minutes as the gyros run down
losing RPM. The real danger here is that the effect is gradual and may
not be noticed by the pilot for some time.

Suction gauge.

The Pitot-Static System

The airspeed indicator (ASI), vertical speed indicator (VSI) and altimeter are all connected to the pitot-static system, although the VSI and altimeter use only static pressure and do not have a pitot pressure pick up.

Pitot and static pressure comes from a PITOT TUBE which is located under the left wing. No checking system is incorporated in the system, and instrument indications in the event of a leak or blockage are outside of the scope of this book. As an option, the pitot tube has a heating element which is activated by a switch in the electrical rocker switch group on the instrument panel, labeled PITOT HEAT. Pitot heat can prevent blockage of the pitot tube in heavy rain or icing. This notwithstanding, it must be remembered that *the PA-28 is not cleared for flight into known icing conditions.* Should the static lines become blocked, it is possible to get static pressure into the system by breaking the face of the vertical speed indicator, and allowing pressure from the cabin to enter the system. This action is rather drastic, probably requiring the use of the fire extinguisher, and should be considered a last resort.

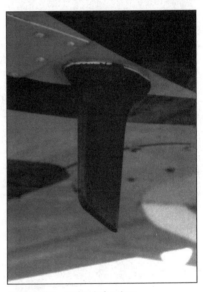

Pitot tube under left wing.

The pitot tube should be checked before flight to ensure that the pitot and static ports are unobstructed. The pitot tube may be protected on the ground with a removable pitot cover. It is important not to blow into either pitot or static vents, because doing so can result in damage to the pressure instruments.

The Heating and Ventilation System

Cabin heating is supplied by a shroud around the engine exhaust system. This allows air, which has entered from an inlet in the rear engine baffles inside the cowling, to be warmed by the exhaust pipes. It can then be directed to outlets in the lower cabin (cabin heat), or at the lower windscreen (defrost) by two levers mounted at the far right instrument panel. The system is very effective once the engine is warm, although its use is governed by a couple of safety factors.

First, the heating system effectively opens a path through the firewall between the engine compartment and the cockpit. For this reason, the cabin heat and defrost are selected OFF before engine start, or if fire is suspected in the engine compartment.

Second, with a system of this type there is always a danger of carbon monoxide (CO) being introduced into the cabin. Carbon monoxide is a gas produced as a by-product of the combustion process. It is colorless, odorless and tasteless, but its effects are potentially fatal. A generally accepted practice is to shut off the heating system if engine fumes (which may contain CO) are thought to be entering the cockpit. This danger arises if a crack or split is present in the exhaust system inside the heating shroud, allowing carbon monoxide to enter the heating system.

The ventilation system consists of cockpit vents, individually controllable, directing fresh air to each seat. Models from between 1970 and 1973 have an additional overhead ventilation system taking fresh air from an inlet in the leading edge of the fin. When the heating system is in use, it is recommended that you operate the fresh air vents to give a comfortable temperature mix. Doing so will help to combat the possible danger of carbon monoxide poisoning, and will prevent the cabin from becoming "stuffy," and possibly inducing drowsiness.

Fresh air inlet in wing leading edge.

Seats and Harnesses

The front seats are adjustable fore and aft. The bar which unlocks the seat position is located below the forward edge of the seat cushion. This bar is raised and then the seat can be moved fore and aft. When the desired position is reached the bar is released and the pilot should check that the seat is positively locked in position. Generally, entry to and exit from the seats is easiest with the seats in the rearmost position. To reach the left seat, the flap lever is best placed fully down (i.e., flaps fully up). To reach the rear seats (where installed), the front seats are best moved to the fully forward position. When the front seats are unoccupied the seat backs can be tilted forward to allow access to the rear seats.

Harness design may vary between different aircraft. In addition to the lap strap, shoulder straps of some description should be installed and their use should be considered mandatory; upper torso restraint has been shown to be a major factor in accident survivability. Final adjustment of the harness should be done when the seat is in the desired location.

Front seats and harnesses.

The baggage area behind the rear seats may be fitted with restraint straps for the securing of items placed in this area. For the Cherokee 140, maximum baggage to be carried in this area is 200 lbs, evenly distributed. On the Cherokee 180, maximum baggage is 125 lbs for models up to 1964, and 200 lbs on models after that date. Attention should be paid to the weight and balance implications of weight in this area. It also must be remembered that for some maneuvers carrying baggage is prohibited.

Doors and Windows

The Cherokee has a single door on the right hand side of the cabin to allow for access to the cabin via the right wing walkway.

The door is latched by pulling it closed, and then using the locking latch at the top of the door. This lever is turned rearwards to latch the door. This latch is almost always difficult to move, particularly for a pilot sitting in the left hand seat.

To open the door, the top latch is released by moving the lever forward, and the small handle at the door front edge is pulled back.

Upper door catch.

Although it is important for the door to be properly latched for flight, the consequences of partial door opening in flight are usually not serious. Where accidents do occur after a door opens in-flight, often the cause is pilot distraction rather than as a direct result of the open door.

When entering and leaving the cabin, the top of the door should not be used as a hand grip to support body weight, as damage to the door and door hinges may result.

Internal door handle.

The 180 models have a rear baggage door fitted to the right side of the fuselage just behind the wing walkway. This door allows for easy loading and unloading of the baggage compartment, and should be checked as closed and locked during the pre-flight checks.

An inward opening "DV WINDOW" is fitted to the left hand window. This window can be opened in flight where visibility through the windscreen has been impaired, or to aid ventilation.

PA-28-180 rear baggage door.

The aircraft design and window area give reasonable visibility, except directly behind. However, the visibility can be degraded by oil smears, insects and other matter accumulating on the windows. For window cleaning, a soft cloth and warm soapy water is recommended; to remove oil and grease, a cloth soaked in kerosene can be used. The use of gasoline, alcohol, thinners and window cleaner sprays is not recommended.

Section 2
Limitations

Dimensions
PA-28 Cherokee 180 1974 Model

PA-28 Cherokee 180

PA-28 Cherokee 140

The "V" Airspeed Code

V_{S0} – (Low end of white arc) Stalling speed with full flaps.

V_{S1} – (Low end of green arc) Stalling speed without flaps.

V_{FE} – Maximum airspeed with flaps extended. Do not extend flaps above this speed, or fly faster than this speed with any flaps extended.

V_A – Design maneuvering speed. Do not make full or abrupt control movements when flying faster than this speed. Design maneuvering speed should not be exceeded when flying in turbulent conditions.

V_{NO} – Maximum structural cruising speed. Do not exceed this speed except in smooth air conditions.

V_{NE} – Never exceed speed. Do not exceed this airspeed under any circumstances.

PA-28-140 Limitations

Airspeed Limitations PA-28-140
(quoted speeds are CALIBRATED airspeed—CAS)

	Knots	MPH
V_{NE}	148	171
V_{NO}	121	140
V_{FE}	100	115
Stalling Speed clean	55	64
Stalling Speed Full Flaps	47	54

INDICATED airspeeds—IAS

	Knots	MPH
V_{NE}	155	178
V_{NO}	124	143
V_A	114	131
V_{FE}	101	116

Airspeed Indicator Markings (CAS) PA-28-140

	Knots	MPH
RED LINE (Never Exceed)	148	171
YELLOW ARC (Caution range)	121 – 148	140 – 171
GREEN ARC (Normal operating range)	55 – 121	64 – 140
WHITE ARC (Flaps extended range)	47 – 100	54 – 115

Maximum Demonstrated
Crosswind Component PA-28-140   17 Knots

Airframe Limitations PA-28-140

Weights	Normal	Utility
Maximum Takeoff Weight	2150 lbs	1950 lbs
Maximum Landing Weight	2150 lbs	1950 lbs
Maximum Baggage Weight	200 lbs	0

Flight Load Factors PA-28-140

	Normal	Utility
Max. Positive load factor:		
FLAPS UP	3.8G	4.4G
FLAPS DOWN	2.0G	2.0G
Max. Negative load factor:		
FLAPS UP	-1.76G	

PA-28-180 Limitations

Airspeed Limitations PA-28-180 (C, D, E, F, G)
(quoted speeds are CALIBRATED airspeed—CAS)

	Knots	MPH
V_{NE}	148	171
V_{NO}	121	140
V_{FE}	100	115
Stalling Speed clean	58	67
Stalling Speed Full Flaps	49	57
INDICATED airspeeds—IAS		
V_{NE}	153	176
V_{NO}	124	143
V_A	114	131
V_{FE}	101	116

Airspeed Indicator Markings (CAS) PA-28-180

	Normal	Utility
RED LINE (Never Exceed)	148	171
YELLOW ARC (Caution range)	121 – 148	140 – 171
GREEN ARC (Normal operating range)	58 – 121	67 – 140
WHITE ARC (Flaps extended range)	49 – 100	57 – 115

**Maximum Demonstrated
Crosswind Component** PA-28-180   17 Knots

Airframe Limitations PA-28-180 (C, D, E, F, G)

Weights	Normal	Utility
Maximum Takeoff Weight	2400 lbs	1950 lbs
Maximum Landing Weight	2400 lbs	1950 lbs
Maximum Baggage Weight	200 lbs	0

Flight Load Factors PA-28-180

	Normal	Utility
Max. Positive load factor:		
FLAPS UP	3.8G	4.4G
FLAPS DOWN	2.0G	2.0G
Max. Negative load factor:		
FLAPS UP	-1.76G	

PA-28-140 and PA-28-180

Engine Limitations

	Tachometer	Instrument Marking
Maximum RPM	2700	Red Line
Normal Operating Range	500 – 2700	Green Arc

Some 180 models may have a specific "RPM to avoid" range—check airplane flight manual.

Oil Limitations

	Oil Temperature	Instrument Marking
Normal operating range	75°* – 245°F	Green Arc
Maximum	245°F	Red Line

* 60°F on PA-28-180 models

	Oil Pressure	Instrument Marking
Normal operating range	60 – 90 psi	Green Arc
Minimum	25 psi	Red Line
Maximum	90 psi	Red Line
Caution range—idle	25 – 60 psi	Yellow Arc

Oil Quantity

	US quart
Capacity	8
Minimum safe quantity	2*

* (+1 quart per hour planned flight)

Fuel System

Fuel Quantity	**US Gal**
Total Capacity	50
Unusable Fuel	0.25*
Usable Fuel	49.75

*180 models 1973 and after unusable fuel is 2.0 US gal.

Fuel Pressure		**Gauge Indication**
Maximum	6.0 psi	Red Line
Minimum	0.5 psi	Red Line
Normal operating range	0.5 – 6.0 psi	Green Arc

Miscellaneous Limitations

Nose Wheel Tire Pressure	24 psi
Main Wheel Tire Pressure	24 psi

Oil Grades

Lycoming approves lubricating oil for the engine that conforms to specification MIL-L-6082 (straight mineral type) and specification MIL-L-22851 (ashless dispersant type).

Straight mineral oil is usually only used when the engine is new, or after maintenance work on the engine. Straight oil grades are known by their weight.

Ashless dispersant oils are more commonly used in service. Ashless dispersant type oil must not be used when the engine is operating on straight mineral oil. It is therefore very important to check which type of oil is currently being used in the engine, and be sure only to add the same type.

Both types of oil are available in different grades, used according to the average ground air temperature. The recommended grades are set out as SAE numbers. The table below shows the recommended grades for various temperature bands.

AVERAGE SURFACE AIR TEMPERATURE	MIL-L-6082 Straight mineral
Above 60°F/16°C	SAE 50
30°F/-1°C – 90°F/32°C	SAE 40
0°F/-18°C – 70°F/21°C	SAE 30
Below 10°F/-12°C	SAE 20
AVERAGE SURFACE AIR TEMPERATURE	**MIL-L-22851 Ashless Dispersant**
Above 60°F/16°C	SAE 50 or SAE 40
30°F/-1°C – 90°F/32°C	SAE 40
0°F/-18°C – 70°F/21°C	SAE 30 or SAE 40
Below 10°F/-12°C	SAE 30

Fuel Grades

The PA-28 Cherokee is certified for use with 100LL fuels.

The table below shows the recommended fuel grades. It is wise to pay attention when your aircraft is being refueled, especially if at an airfield new to you. More than one pilot has found out that piston engines designed for AVGAS do not run very well on turbine fuel (Jet A-1). To help guard against this eventuality AVGAS fueling points carry a RED sticker, and turbine fuel fueling points a BLACK sticker.

APPROVED FUEL GRADES
100LL
100L
100

Section 3
Handling the Piper
PA-28 Cherokee

Engine Starting

Starting the Cherokee presents no problems, but the ambient conditions and engine temperature are the prime factors to be considered. A cold engine will require between 2 and 4 primes; a hot engine should not

 require any priming at all. The throttle is set to one-quarter open (that is, 1/4-inch in), with the mixture rich and fuel set to the tank with the lowest quantity (unless of course that tank is empty). "Pumping" the throttle during starting should be avoided, as the accelerator pump will cause fuel to pool in the intake, causing a fire risk.

 Cranking the starter should be limited to 30 seconds at a time due to the danger of the starter motor overheating. After a prolonged period of engine cranking without a successful start, the starter should be allowed a few minutes to cool before a further attempt is made. The starter should not be operated after engine start, as damage to the starter may result.

 After start, the oil pressure should register within 30 seconds. Should the oil pressure not register, the engine should be shut down without delay. Readings on the suction gauge and ammeter are also usually checked after engine start.

Starting With a Suspected Flooded Engine

An over-primed (flooded) engine will be indicated by weak intermittent firing, and puffs of black smoke from the exhaust. If it is suspected that the engine is flooded (over-primed) the throttle should be opened fully and the mixture moved to idle cut-off. If the engine starts, the mixture should be moved to full rich and the throttle retarded to the normal position.

Starting In Cold Ambient Conditions (below 0°C)

Failure to start due to an under-primed engine is most likely to occur in cold conditions with a cold engine. An under-primed engine will not fire at all, and additional priming is necessary. Starting in cold temperatures will be more difficult due to several factors. The oil will be more viscous, the battery may lose up to half of its capacity, and the fuel will not vaporize readily. A greater number of primes will be required, external power may be needed to supplement the aircraft battery, and pre-heat may be necessary in very low temperatures.

Taxiing

In the first few feet of taxiing, a brake check is normally carried out, followed by steering and differential brake checks. It is common practice to check the hand-operated brake lever in addition to the toe brakes (if these are installed). The direct link, via steering rods, from the rudder pedals to the nose wheel makes the Cherokee easy to steer accurately, although on earlier models the steering is quite heavy to operate. Use of differential brakes can give a very small turning circle; increased power is often required when using prolonged differential braking. Where toe brakes are not installed, the brake lever can be used in conjunction with full rudder to reduce turn radius. When taxiing with a crosswind, "opposite rudder" will be required, up to full deflection. For example, with a cross-wind from the left, up to full right rudder may be required as the aircraft tries to "weathervane" into the wind. In this situation differential braking will also aid directional control.

The figure below shows recommended control wheel positions when taxiing with the prevailing wind from the directions shown.

Power and Pre-Takeoff Checks

The aircraft is usually positioned into the wind to aid engine cooling, and before the power checks start, the oil temperature should be in the green arc.

The engine is generally run up to 2,000 RPM, with the fuel tank with greatest quantity selected (the same tank should be used for takeoff). At this RPM, the carburetor heat is checked, and a small drop in RPM should be noted. The subject of carburetor icing is covered in Section 4, but an important point to note is that the inlet for the "hot" air is unfiltered. Therefore, dust, grass, etc. may well enter the engine when "hot" air is selected, leading to increased engine wear. For this reason the use of carburetor heat should be kept to the minimum necessary while on the ground.

The magnetos are checked individually, with no more than 3 seconds on each magneto recommended to avoid plug fouling. A small drop in RPM is the norm and shows that the ignition system is functioning properly. No RPM drop at all when operating on one magneto may well indicate a malfunction in the ignition system, and the possibility that one or both magnetos are staying "live." An excessive drop in RPM when operating on one magneto, especially when accompanied by rough running, may indicate fouled spark plugs or a faulty magneto. If fouled plugs are suspected it may be possible to clear the problem. The engine is set to about 2,000 RPM with magnetos on BOTH, and the mixture leaned to give the "peak" RPM. This should be held for about 10 seconds, then the mixture returned to full rich and the magnetos rechecked.

WARNING: Excessive power setting and over-lean mixture settings should be avoided during this procedure. If the problem does not clear, the aircraft should be considered unserviceable.

The engine gauges, together with the suction gauge and ammeter, are checked at 2,000 RPM for normal indications. The throttle is then closed, and the engine should idle smoothly at about 500 – 750 RPM.

Takeoff

Normally, takeoff is made with the mixture in the full RICH position. At high elevation airfields (above about 3,000 feet MSL), it may be necessary to lean the mixture before takeoff to give maximum power.

For all takeoffs care must be taken to ensure that the feet remain clear of the toe brakes (where these are installed). It should also be positively confirmed that the brake lever is fully OFF.

At the start of the takeoff run (as at all other times), the throttle should be opened smoothly and progressively. Rapid opening of the throttle should be specifically avoided because of the danger of a "rich mixture out." The normal rotation speed is 73 mph, with a climb speed of 85 mph, dependent on conditions and operator procedures. In crosswind conditions, the rotation speed should be increased to ensure full control immediately after takeoff. For "short field" takeoffs, the use of 2 stages of flaps (25°) is common practice.

On rough surfaces particularly, it is important to protect the nose wheel by keeping weight off it during the takeoff run, although "over-rotating" should be avoided as this will lengthen the takeoff run—and ruin the view ahead!

Climbing

An airspeed in the region of 85 mph will give the best rate of climb after takeoff. The best angle of climb (the best increase in height for the shortest distance traveled over the ground), can be obtained at 78 mph with 25° of flaps lowered. During climbing it is important to monitor the engine gauges, as the engine is operating at a high power setting but with a reduced cooling airflow compared to cruising flight. Lookout ahead is impaired by the high nose attitude, and it is common practice to "weave" the nose periodically during the climb to visually check the area ahead.

Engine Handling

Engine rough running can be caused by a number of factors. It should be remembered that the majority of engine failures in light aircraft are caused by pilot error. After carburetor icing, fuel exhaustion (running out of fuel) or fuel starvation (i.e., fuel on-board but not reaching the engine) are common causes of engine failure. Having sufficient fuel on board to complete the flight is a point of basic airmanship, and is accomplished through proper flight planning and thorough pre-flight checks. Keeping the fuel tanks in balance and monitoring the fuel system are a part of the cruise checks. In the Cherokee, fuel starvation may occur if the engine driven fuel pump fails. In this instance, the use of the electric fuel pump should restore the fuel supply to the engine and allow for a diversion to be made.

Regular monitoring of the engine instruments may forewarn of an impending problem. HIGH OIL TEMPERATURE may indicate a faulty gauge, if not accompanied by a corresponding drop in oil pressure. As with most instances, the action to be taken will depend on the pilots judgment of the situation at the time. A reasonable course of action would be a diversion to a suitable airfield, while remaining alert to the possibility of a sudden engine failure. *Where high oil temperature is accompanied by a low oil pressure, engine failure may very well be imminent, and the pilot should act accordingly.* Such a situation might occur during a prolonged slow climb in hot conditions. In this instance, increasing the airspeed to provide more cooling, and reducing power if possible, may restore oil temperature to normal. In the event of a LOW OIL PRESSURE reading, accompanied by a normal oil temperature reading, gauge failure may be the culprit, and the pilot can consider actions similar to those for an oil temperature gauge failure.

Stalling

A Reminder: The information in this section is no substitute for flight instruction under the guidance of a flight instructor familiar with the aircraft and its characteristics.

The Cherokee is straightforward in its stalling behavior. The stall warning light activates 5 to 10 mph above the stall airspeed. It is electrically operated, and so it is inoperative with the master switch off, or with a faulty electrical system. The actual stall speed can be affected by many factors including the aircraft weight and center of gravity position. The use of power will lower the stalling speed, while turning flight raises the stall speed. The use of flaps, power, or turning flight considerably increases the chances of a wing drop at the stall. When practicing stalls, the possibility of a wing drop can be reduced by keeping the aircraft coordinated during the approach to the stall. Typical height loss for a full stall with a conventional recovery (using power) is about 200 feet. A very gentle stall and absence of wing drop characterize the Cherokee stall.

Stalling in the Cherokee is usually achieved with the control wheel held fully aft. In this position the control wheel moves upwards, and it is possible to have this movement blocked by one or both of the front seat occupants, particularly if they have the seat in the forward position. The pre-takeoff "full and free control movement" check will help avoid this possibility.

Spins

Always check aircraft flight manual before intentional spinning.

A Reminder: The information in this section is no substitute for flight instruction from a flight instructor familiar with the aircraft and its characteristics.

The Cherokee is approved for intentional spinning when operating in the utility category.

It is very important to understand that spins (and some other maneuvers) are only approved with the aircraft in the utility category. The principal limitations are maximum weight 1,950 lbs, and an aft CG limit of 86.5 inches. The Cherokee CG position is not too sensitive to the front seat occupants, as the seats are located close to the center of gravity. The CG position is, however, *very* sensitive to the fuel weight, which is further aft of the normal CG position. Without going into exact figures, a reduced fuel load *will* be necessary to ensure the aircraft is in the utility category. It's very important to know this quirk of the Cherokee. For operations in the utility category, a proper weight and balance check should be made, with particular reference to the fuel load. Fatal accidents—involving experienced instructors—have occurred when Cherokees have been spun with a fuel load that caused the CG to exceed the aft limit even by only a small amount.

As with stalling, several factors can effect the behavior of the aircraft in the spin. It is quite possible to devote a whole book just to this subject, and it is not the intention here to write a textbook on spinning; however, some points are worthy of mention. The weight of the aircraft (and particularly the CG position as discussed) has a noticeable effect on the spin. High weights tend to extend the spin recovery due to the increase in inertia. The position of the ailerons is important in spinning. The ailerons should be held NEUTRAL throughout the spin and recovery.

The spin is normal, and standard recovery action is effective. In fact, when properly loaded (i.e., in the utility category) the main problem is in persuading the aircraft to enter a proper spin in the first place.

The recommended spin recovery is as follows: (operator techniques may vary)

• Check ailerons neutral and throttle closed.

• Apply and maintain full opposite rudder (opposite to the direction of spin).

• Move the control wheel forward until the stall is broken and the spin stops.

• When rotation stops center the rudder and recover from the ensuing dive.

Descent

The descent may be powered or glide. For the glide, a speed of about 85 mph is standard. Where flaps are used the rate of descent increases, the initial lowering of flaps leads to a definite nose down pitching and reduced airspeed. The low power settings usually used during the descent, and a possible prolonged descent into warmer air, provide ideal conditions for carburetor icing, full carburetor heat should be used where necessary. In a glide descent, power should be added for short periods throughout the descent to help prevent spark plug fouling, rapid cylinder cooling, and of course, carburetor icing.

Landing

For the approach to landing the mixture should be fully RICH (unless landing at a very high elevation airfield), the electric fuel pump should be on, and the tank with the most fuel selected. The Cherokee is not a difficult aircraft to land, although the stabilator does tend to be heavy in feel during the flare, particularly with the Cherokee 180s. Despite the relative ease of landing, the Cherokees (as with many other light aircraft) appear year after year in landing accident reports. It is rare that anybody is hurt in these accidents, but the reports seem surprisingly similar:

"Piper PA-28-140 Cherokee —. Nose gear collapsed following a heavy landing at —."

"Piper PA-28-180 Cherokee —. Nose gear collapsed on landing at —."

"Piper PA-28-140 Cherokee —. Following a bounce on landing at — airport, the aircraft then porpoised, striking the nose wheel on the runway....."

The nose wheel is nowhere near as strong as the main gear, but there is no need for its strength to be tested if a proper approach and landing technique is used. Approach speed for a normal approach with flaps is about 85 mph, usually a little higher for a flapless approach. Incorrect approach speed is a primary cause of "ballooning," which often leads to bouncing. Bouncing also occurs where the aircraft is allowed to touch down at too high a speed, usually in a level attitude rather than a nose-up attitude. The correct action in either a "balloon" or a bounce is to GO AROUND without delay. The correct landing technique is to approach at the proper speed, "flare" or "hold off," close the throttle, and gradually raise the nose to ensure a slow touchdown speed on the *main wheels first*, with the nose wheel still off the ground. As the aircraft slows down, correct use of the stabilator means the nose wheel is allowed to gently contact the surface some time after the initial main wheel contact. Again, there is no substitute for flight instruction in the proper technique with a flight instructor.

The go-around in the Cherokee does not provide any problems, even with full flaps extended. The trim change when applying full power is manageable, and although the aircraft will climb with full flaps extended it is common practice to raise flaps to the second stage (25°) as part of the immediate go-around actions.

Parking and Tie Down

The aircraft is generally parked into the wind; it is good practice to stop with the nose wheel straight so that the rudder is not deflected. All switches should be off, and the doors closed. In extremely cold weather it may be advisable *not* to set the parking brake as moisture may freeze the brakes; in addition, the parking brake should not be set if there is reason to believe that the brakes are overheated. If for any reason the parking brake is not set, the wheels should be "chocked."

A well protected and tied down Cherokee.

When tying down the aircraft the following technique is recommended:

- Park aircraft into the wind with the flaps retracted.
- Secure the flight controls by looping the seat belt through the control wheel.
- Tie ropes, cables or chains to the wing tie-down points and secure to ground anchor points.
- If desired, a rope (not cable or chain) can be secured to the nose gear and secured to a ground anchor point.
- A rope can be passed through the tail tie-down point and each end secured at a 45° angle each side of the tail.
- External control locks may be advisable in strong or gusty wind conditions.

It is also prudent to use a pitot cover, particularly if the aircraft will be left unattended for some time.

Section 4
Mixture and Carburetor Icing Supplement

Carburetor Icing

Almost certainly the most common cause of engine rough-running, and complete engine failure, is carburetor icing. Despite this, carburetor icing remains a widely misunderstood subject. Many pilots' knowledge of the subject is limited to a feeling that the carburetor heat should be used regularly in flight, without really knowing the symptoms of carburetor icing or the conditions most likely to cause its formation.

How Carburetor Icing Forms

IMPACT ICING occurs when ice forms over the external air inlet (air filter) and inside the induction system leading to the carburetor. This type of icing occurs with the temperature below 0°C while flying in clouds, or in precipitation (i.e., rain, sleet or snow). These conditions are also conducive to airframe icing, and the aircraft is *not cleared for flight into known icing conditions,* which clearly these are. So, assuming the aircraft is operated legally within its limitations, this form of icing should not occur, and is not considered further.

CARBURETOR ICING is caused by a temperature drop inside the carburetor, which can happen even in conditions where other forms of icing will not occur. The causes of this temperature drop are twofold:

1. FUEL ICING—the evaporation of fuel inside the carburetor. Liquid fuel changes to fuel vapor and mixes with the induction air causing a large temperature drop. If the temperature inside the carburetor falls below 0°C, water vapor in the atmosphere condenses into ice, usually on the walls of the carburetor passage adjacent to the fuel jet, and on the throttle valve. Generally, fuel icing is responsible for around 70% of the temperature drop in the carburetor.

Throttle valve

Ice build-up

2. THROTTLE ICING—the temperature loss caused by the acceleration of air and consequent pressure drop around the throttle valve. This effect may again take the temperature below 0°C, and water vapor in the inlet air will condense into ice on the throttle valve. This practical effect is a demonstration of Bernoulli's Principle.

As fuel and throttle icing generally occur together, they are known just as carburetor icing.

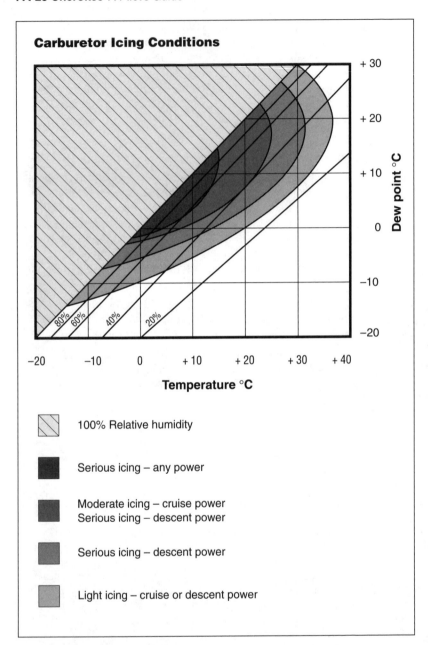

Carburetor Icing Conditions

100% Relative humidity

Serious icing – any power

Moderate icing – cruise power
Serious icing – descent power

Serious icing – descent power

Light icing – cruise or descent power

Conditions Likely to Lead to Carburetor Icing

Two criteria govern the likelihood of carburetor icing conditions: the AIR TEMPERATURE and the RELATIVE HUMIDITY.

The ambient air temperature is important, *but not because the temperature needs to be below 0°C, or even close to freezing.* The temperature drop in the carburetor can be up to 30°C, so carburetor icing can (and does) occur in hot ambient conditions. It is no wonder carburetor icing is sometimes referred to as refrigeration icing. Carburetor icing is considered a possibility within the temperature range of -10°C to +30°C.

The relative humidity (a measure of the water content of the atmosphere) is a major factor. The greater the water content in the atmosphere (the higher the relative humidity), the greater the risk of carburetor icing. That said, the relative humidity (RH) does not to have to be 100% (i.e., visible water droplets—cloud, rain), for carburetor icing to occur. Carburetor icing is considered a possibility at relative humidity values as low as 30%. Herein lies perhaps the real danger of carburetor icing, that it can occur in such a wide range of conditions. Obviously the pilot must be alert to the possibility of carburetor icing at just about all times. Flight in or near clouds, or in other visible moisture (i.e., rain) might be an obvious cause of carburetor icing, but—*visible moisture does not need to be present for carburetor icing to occur.*

Symptoms of Carburetor Icing

In this aircraft, fitted with a fixed pitch propeller, the symptoms of carburetor icing are straightforward. A loss of RPM will be the first symptom, although this is often first noticed as a loss of altitude. As the icing becomes more serious, engine rough-running may occur.

Carburetor icing is often detected during the use of the carburetor heat. Normally when the carburetor heat is used, a small drop in RPM occurs; when the control is returned to cold (off) the RPM restores to the same as before the use of carburetor heat. If the RPM restores to a figure higher than before the carburetor heat was used, it can be assumed that some form of carburetor icing was present.

Use of Carburetor Heat

Apart from the normal check of carburetor heat during the power checks, it may be necessary to use the carburetor heat on the ground if carburetor icing is suspected. Safety considerations apart, the use of carburetor heat on the ground should be kept to a minimum, because the hot air inlet is unfiltered and sand or dust can enter the engine, increasing engine wear.

Carburetor icing is generally considered to be very unlikely with the engine operating at above 75% power, i.e., during the takeoff and climb. Carburetor heat should not be used with the engine operating at above 75% power (i.e., full throttle) as detonation may occur. Detonation is the uncontrolled burning of fuel in the cylinders, literally an explosion, and will cause serious damage to the engine very quickly. Apart from the danger of detonation, the use of carburetor heat reduces the power the engine produces. In any situation where full power is required (i.e., takeoff, climb, go-around) the carburetor heat must be off (cold).

Very few operators recommend the use of anything other than FULL carburetor heat. A normal carburetor icing check will involve leaving the carburetor heat on (hot) for 5 to 10 seconds, although the pilot may wish to vary this dependent on the conditions. The use of carburetor heat does increase the fuel consumption, and this may be a factor to consider if the aircraft is being flown towards the limit of its range/endurance in possible carburetor icing conditions.

With carburetor icing present, the use of carburetor heat may lead to a large drop in RPM, with rough running. The instinctive reaction is to put the carburetor heat back to cold (off), and quickly—this is, however, the wrong action. Chances are this rough running is a good thing, and the carburetor heat should be left on (hot) until the rough running clears, and the RPM rises. In this instance, the use of carburetor heat has melted a large amount of accumulated icing, and the melted ice is passing through the engine causing temporary rough running.

Care should be taken when flying in very cold ambient conditions (below -10°C). In these conditions the use of carburetor heat may actually raise

Carburetor heat control

Carburetor heat control
COLD

Carburetor heat control
HOT

Carburetor

Carburetor

Air
filter

Hot
air

Air
filter

Hot
air

Overboard

Overboard

the temperature in the carburetor to that most conducive to carburetor icing. Generally, when the temperature in the carburetor is below -8°C, moisture forms directly into ice crystals which pass through the engine.

The RPM loss normally associated with the use of carburetor heat is caused by the reduced density of the hot air entering the carburetor, leading to an over-rich mixture entering the engine. If the carburetor heat has to be left constantly on (hot)—i.e., flight in heavy rain and clouds—it may be advisable to lean the mixture in order to maintain RPM and smooth engine running.

It is during the descent (and particularly the glide descent) that carburetor icing is most likely to occur. The position of the throttle valve (i.e., almost closed) is a contributory factor, and even though the carburetor heat is normally applied throughout a glide descent, the low engine power will reduce the temperature of the hot air selected with the carburetor heat control. In addition, a loss of power may not be readily noticed, as the propeller is likely to windmill even after a complete loss of power. A full loss of power may only be apparent when the throttle is opened at the bottom of the descent. This is one good reason for opening the throttle to "clear the engine" at intervals during a glide descent.

The Mixture Control

The aircraft is provided with a mixture control, so that the pilot can adjust the fuel/air mixture entering the engine when necessary. The cockpit mixture control operates a needle valve between the float bowl and the main metering jet. This valve controls the fuel flow to the main metering jet to adjust the mixture. With the mixture control in the idle cut-off position (full lean), the valve is fully closed.

Reasons for Adjusting the Mixture

Correct leaning of the engine will enable the engine to be operated at its most efficient in terms of fuel consumption. With the increased use of 100LL fuel, leaning is also important to reduce spark plug fouling.

The most efficient engine operation is obtained with a fuel/air ratio of about 1:15; that is, 1 part fuel to 15 parts air. In fact, with the mixture set to full rich, the system is designed to give a slightly richer mixture than ideal; typically about 1:12. This slightly over-rich mixture reduces the possibility of pre-ignition or detonation, and aids cylinder cooling.

As altitude increases, the air density decreases. Above about 3,000 feet the reduced air density can lead to an over-rich mixture. If the mixture becomes excessively rich, power will be lost, rough running may be evident and ultimately engine failure will occur due to a "rich out." It is for

Effects of Mixture Adjustment

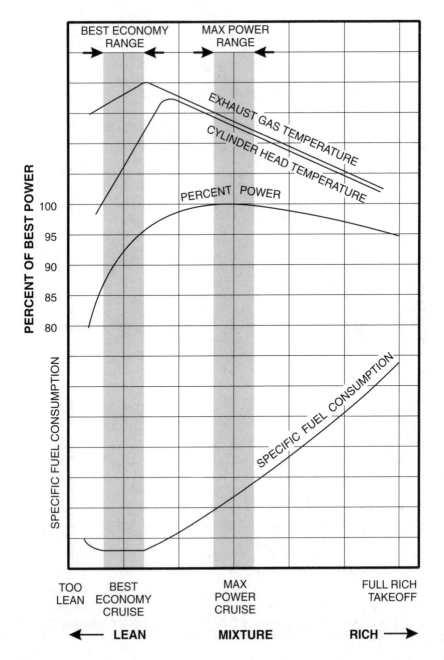

this reason that the mixture control is provided to ensure the correct fuel/ air ratio; typically it is used when cruising above 3,000 feet.

The flight manuals for some older aircraft recommend leaning only above 5,000 feet. However, with the increasing use of AVGAS 100LL, and the plug fouling problems sometimes associated with 100LL, most operators recommend leaning once above 3,000 feet.

Use of the Mixture Control

For takeoff and climb, the mixture should be full rich; the only exception is operation from a high density altitude airport, when leaning may be necessary to ensure the availability of maximum power. On reaching a cruising altitude above about 3,000 feet, the cruise power should be set, and then leaning can be carried out. (Note: Generally, leaning with over 75% power set is not recommended.) If climbing above about 5,000 feet, full throttle will be less than 75% power on a normally aspirated engine, and so leaning may be permissible to maintain smooth running.

Assuming that there is no Exhaust Gas Temperature (EGT) gauge and no cylinder head temperature gauge, the primary instrument to watch when leaning is the RPM gauge (tachometer).

To lean the engine, the recommended power setting (RPM) is set with the throttle. Next, with a constant throttle setting, the mixture control is slowly moved back (leaned). If leaning is required, the RPM will increase slowly, peak, and then decrease as the mixture is leaned. If leaning is continued, the engine will ultimately run rough and lose power.

If the mixture is set to achieve peak RPM, the maximum power mixture has been achieved.

If the mixture is set to give a tachometer reading 25 to 50 RPM less than peak RPM on the "lean" side, the best economy mixture has been achieved. This setting is the one that many aircraft manufacturers recommend, and their performance claims are based on such a procedure.

Using a mixture that is too lean is a false economy, and will lead to serious engine damage sooner or later. Detonation (an uncontrolled explosive combustion of the mixture in the cylinder) is particularly dangerous, and can lead to an engine failure in a very short time. The use of a full rich mixture during full power operations is specifically to ensure engine cooling and guard against detonation.

For any change in operating conditions (altitude, power setting) the mixture will need to be reset. It is particularly important that the mixture is set to full rich before increasing the power setting.

During a descent from a high altitude, the mixture will gradually become too lean if not enriched, leading to excessive cylinder temperatures, power loss and ultimately engine failure. Normally the mixture is set to full rich prior to landing, unless operating at a high elevation airfield.

Moving the mixture to the full lean position—ICO (idle cut-off)—closes the needle valve, and so stops fuel supply to the main metering jet. This is the normal method for shutting down the engine and ensures that no unburned fuel mixture is left in the engine.

Section 5
Expanded PA-28
Pre-Flight Checklist

A proper pre-flight check will avoid missing the obvious (plenty of pilots have tried to get airborne with tow-bars or tie-downs still attached) …

…or the more subtle (under-wing mud and stone damage).

Approaching Aircraft

1. Check for and remove any tie-downs, external control locks, pitot cover and wheel chocks.

2. Look for any oil and fuel spillage from aircraft.

3. Remove any ice and frost from *all* surfaces.

4. Check for access to taxiways, obstructions, loose gravel, etc.

5. Look to see if aircraft is on a level surface. This may effect the visual check of fuel quantity.

In Cabin

1. **Internal Control locks and covers** .... Remove, stow securely.

2. **Parking Brake** .... Check ON with locking plate in.

3. **Magneto Switch** .... Check OFF and Key Out —*otherwise the propeller is live and lethal.*

4. **Master Switch** .... On. Turn on pitot heater, anti-collision beacon, landing light and navigation lights. Leave cockpit and check:

5. **Stall Warning Vane** .... Move gently forward to check.

6. **Pitot Heat** .... Check with fingers that pitot tube is warm (it may take a minute or so to warm up).

7. **Anti-Collision Beacon** .... Check operation (rotating red light on fin).

8. **Landing/Nav lights** .... Check. The navigation lights colors are: PORT (Left) – red; STARBOARD (Right) – green; REAR (Tail) – white

   Return to cockpit and turn off electrical services.

9. **Fuel Selector Valve** .... Turn On—Check quantity gauges.

10. **Master Switch** .... Off.

11. **Flaps** .... Lower to second stage (25°).

12. **Trim Wheel** .... Check position neutral using indicator.

13. **First Aid Kit** .... Check in position, secure.

14. **Fire Extinguisher** .... Check in position, secure and serviceable (gauge at top should be in green arc).

15. **Cockpit** .... Check for and remove/stow any loose articles.

16. **Upon leaving cockpit *do not* tread on flap surface.**

External

Begin at rear of wing. This should also be where you complete your checks.

Starboard Wing

1. **Flap**................................Check upper and lower surface condition. Particularly check inner lower surface for caked mud or stone damage from wheels. Check linkages secure and greased.

2. **Aileron**...........................Check upper and lower surface condition, linkages and hinges secure. With fingers inside hinge line (hold the aileron with other hand), check balance weight is secure. Check full and free movement—*Do not use force.*

3. **Wing Tip** ...... Check condition, security. Navigation light unbroken. (This area is particularly vulnerable to hanger damage.)

4. **Wing Surface** ....Check upper and lower surface condition.

5. **Wing Leading Edge** ....Check for dents along entire length.

6. **Fuel Tank** ....Check quantity visually, resecure cap. Check fuel vent unblocked. Take fuel drain sample from under tank if necessary—check for correct color, water bubbles or sediment. Check that drain is not leaking.

Starboard Landing Gear

1. **Tire** .... Check for tread and general condition. Check for correct inflation. Check alignment of creep marks.

2. **Hydraulic Lines** .... Check for leaks (red fluid).

3. **Disc Brake** .... Should be shiny, not rusty or pitted.

4. **Oleo** .... Check for correct extension. Look for mud or stone damage on wing and flap surface near landing gear.

Front Fuselage and Engine

1. **Starboard Cowling** .... Open engine compartment, check oil level, *do not* overtighten dipstick on resecuring. Check cowling.

2. **Windscreen** .... Should be clean and insect free; OAT probe secure.

3. **Nose Gear** .... Check oleo extension, linkages, nuts and split pins secure.

4. **Nose Wheel** .... Check for tread and general condition. Check for correct inflation. Check alignment of creep marks.

5. **Landing light** .... Check for damage.

6. **Propeller** .... Look for cracks or chips, especially leading edge. Check spinner secure and condition good. *Do not move or swing propeller.*

7. **Port Cowling** .... Open cowling and check brake fluid level. Check engine compartment (i.e., HT leads secure, etc.). Resecure cowling. Take fuel sample. Check that fuel drain is not leaking.

Port Landing Gear

1. **Tire** .... Check for tread and general condition. Check for correct inflation. Look for alignment of creep marks.

2. **Hydraulic Lines** .... Check for leaks (red fluid).

3. **Disc Brake** .... Should be shiny, not rusty or pitted.

4. **Oleo** .... Check extension. Look for mud or stone damage on wing and flap surface near landing gear.

Port Wing

1. **Fuel Tank** .... Check quantity visually, resecure cap. Take fuel drain sample if necessary. Check that drain is not leaking.

2. **Wing Surface** .... Check upper and lower surface condition.

3. **Wing Leading Edge** .... Check for dents along entire length. Check pitot tube perforations unblocked—*Do not blow into pitot tube.*

4. **Wing Tip** .... Check condition, security, navigation light unbroken.

5. **Aileron** .... Check upper and lower surface condition, linkages and hinges secure, balance weight (inside wing tip) secure. Remember to watch for aileron movement while checking inside hinge line. Check full and free movement gently—*Do not use force.*

6. **Flap** .... Check upper and lower surface condition especially near landing gear. Check linkages secure and greased.

Port Fuselage

1. **Windows** .... Check clean and uncracked.

2. **Skin** .... Check general surface condition upper and lower. Look for wrinkles, dents or punctures.

3. **Radio Antennas** .... Check secure.

4. **Tail Fin** .... Check skin condition, especially fairings. Check antennas and rotating beacon secure.

5. **Rudder** .... Check condition, linkages secure and greased, nuts and split pins secure, Nav light unbroken. *Do not attempt to force rudder movement.*

6. **Stabilator** .... Check upper and lower surface condition. Check linkages and split pins. Check full and free movement—*Do not use force.* Ensure anti-balance tab moves in correct sense. Check other side of tail fin.

Starboard Fuselage

1. **Skin** .... Check general surface condition, upper and lower, look for any wrinkles, dents or punctures.

2. **Radio Antennas** .... Check secure. Do not tread on flap surface.

3. **Cockpit Door and Baggage Door** .... Check latches and secure hinges.

4. **Windows** .... Check clean and uncracked.

Important

Remember: Full reference must be made to airplane flight manual, Pilot's Operating Handbook, flight school syllabus, etc., for all normal and emergency procedures.

If in doubt—ask

Section 6
Loading and Performance

Loading

Aircraft loading can be divided into two areas, the aircraft weight and the center of gravity (CG) position.

The aircraft must be loaded so that its weight is below the certified maximum takeoff weight (2,150 lbs for the PA-28-140 or 2,400 lbs for the PA-28-180). The weight limit is set primarily as a function of the lifting capability of the aircraft, which is largely determined by the wing design and engine power of the aircraft. Operating the aircraft when it is over-weight will adversely effect the aircraft handling and performance, such as:

Increased takeoff speed and slower acceleration

Increased runway length required for takeoff

Reduced rate of climb

Reduced maximum altitude capability

Reduced range and endurance

Reduction in maneuverability and controllability

Increased stall speed

Increased approach and landing speed

Increased runway length required for landing

The aircraft must also be loaded to ensure that its center of gravity is within set limits, normally defined as a forward and aft limit in inches aft of the datum. The forward limit is determined by the amount of elevator control available at landing speed; the aft limit is determined by the stability and controllability of the aircraft while maneuvering. Attempted flight with the CG position outside of the set limits (either forward or aft) will lead to control difficulties, and possibly loss of control of the aircraft.

When loading the aircraft it is standard practice to calculate the weight and CG position of the aircraft at the same time, commonly known as the weight and balance calculation. Before going further it must be empha-sized that the following examples are provided for illustrative purposes only. Each *individual* aircraft has an *individual* weight and balance record that is valid only for that aircraft, and is dependent among other things on the equipment installed in the aircraft. If the aircraft has any major modification, repair or new equipment installed, a new weight and balance record will be produced. Therefore, for any loading or perfor-mance calculations, you must use the documents for the specific aircraft you will be using. As well as setting out limits, the aircraft documents will also give arms for each item of loading. The arm is a distance from the aircraft datum to the item. The weight multiplied by its arm gives its moment. Thus a set weight will have a greater moment the further away it is from the datum.

Weight and Center of Gravity Record

Produced by:

Grosvenor Aviation Services (Engineering) Limited

Aircraft Type:

Piper PA38-112

Nationality and Registration Marks:

N-BGRR

Constructor's Serial Number:

78A0336

Maximum Permissible Weight:

1670 lbs

Maximum Landing Weight:

1670 lbs

Center of Gravity Limits:

Refer to Flight Manual Rep No. FAA 2126

All arms are distances in inches either fore or aft of datum.

Part "A" Basic Weight

The basic weight of this aircraft as calculated from Planeweighs Limited Report No. 1034 weighed on 08.07.88. at Manchester Airport is: **1182 lbs**

The center of gravity of aircraft in the same condition (aft of the datum) is: **74.66 inches**

The total Moment about the datum in this condition in lb inches is: **88254.45**

The DATUM referred to is defined in the Flight Manual, which is **66.25 inches** forward of wing leading edge.

The basic weight includes the weight of 12 lbs unusable fuel and 15 lbs of oil and the weight of items indicated in Appendix 1 which comprises the list of basic equipment carried.

Each individual aircraft has an individual weight and balance record, valid only for that aircraft.

ARM (95) x WEIGHT (204) = MOMENT (19,380)

The operating weight of the aircraft can be split into two categories:

EMPTY WEIGHT—the weight of the aircraft, including unusable fuel; normally this includes full oil as well. The weight and CG position of the aircraft in this condition will be noted in the weight and balance record.

USEFUL LOAD—weight of pilot, co-pilot, passengers, usable fuel and baggage. Again, the weight and balance record will give an arm for each of these loads.

Mathematical Weight and Balance Calculation

With this method of calculation the weights of each item are listed together with their arm. Addition of all the weights is the first step, to ensure that the resulting figure is within the maximum permitted. Assuming this is the case, the balance can then be calculated. For each item (except for the empty weight where the calculation is done already on the weight and balance record) the weight is multiplied by the arm, to give a moment. Normally the arm is aft of the datum, to give a positive figure. If the arm quoted is forward of the datum the moment will be negative (obviously, the weight is *not* deducted from the weight calculation). All the moments are then added together, to give the total moment, and this figure is then divided by the total weight. The resulting figure will be the position of the CG, which can be checked to ensure it is within the set limits. The weight and CG position can be plotted on a graph in the flight manual. If the plotted position is within the "envelope," the weight and CG position are within limits.

It is obviously important for the pilot to be certain whether the aircraft needs to operated in the NORMAL or UTILITY categories. The aircraft flight manual will advise which maneuvers can only be carried out when the aircraft is in the utility category (e.g., spinning). Operation in the utility category is defined as a reduced weight (1,950 lbs) and different CG limits. In addition, baggage in the rear baggage area is not permitted. The critical importance of the fuel load in the calculation of CG position for utility category operations should be remembered. As an illustration, here is a practical example for a well-equipped Cherokee 140.

Example:

Empty Weight: Aircraft N19367 (PA-28-140)
From the weight and balance record for this aircraft, weight is 1,449.16 lbs

Useful Load: Pilot 140 lbs
Co-Pilot 140 lbs
Fuel 15 US gal @ 6.0 lbs per US gal = 90 lbs

Although at this stage you can simply add together the weights to check the total weight, it is more common to make up a table to check weight *and* balance. Using the information above, and the arms from the weight and balance record, we can make up a table to calculate the moment for each item (remembering that weight x arm gives the moment).

Most Cherokee flight manuals do not contain a weight and center of gravity graph. Therefore we have drawn graphs using data from the flight manuals, for a PA-28-140 and PA-28-180. These graphs are purely illustrative and are not to be used for Center of Gravity calculations.

ITEM	WEIGHT (lbs)	ARM (in)	MOMENT (lb-in)
Empty Weight: the weight, arm and moment are listed in the weight and balance record.			
N19367	1,449.16	86.13	124,816.00
Useful Load			
Pilot	140.0	85.5	11,970.00
Passenger	140.0	85.5	11,970.00
Fuel	90.0	95.0	8,550.00
Total Weight 1,819.16		Total Moment 157,306.00	

The total weight is below the maximum utility limit, and so it is acceptable.

Dividing the total moment by the total weight gives the Center of Gravity position:

$$\frac{157,306}{1,819.16} = 86.47 \text{ inches aft of datum}$$

When this weight and CG position is plotted on the relevant graph, it can be seen that the aircraft is loaded to be within the UTILITY category. However, you can see from the weight of the pilots and the small quantity of fuel how difficult it is to properly load the aircraft to the utility category.

Now an example of normal category operations in a Cherokee 180:

ITEM	WEIGHT (lbs)	ARM (in)	MOMENT (lb-in)
Empty Weight: the weight, arm and moment are listed in the weight and balance record (for 19258 only unusable oil is included here).			
N19258	1,405	86.1	120,970.50
Useful Load			
Pilot	160	85.5	13,680.00
Passenger	160	85.5	13,680.00
Fuel (Full)	302	95.0	28,690.00
Usable Oil	15	32.5	487.50
2x Rear Seat Pax	300	118.1	35,430.00
Rear baggage	40	142.8	5,712.00
Total Weight	2,382	Total Moment	218,650.00

The total weight is below the maximum permitted (2,400 lbs).

Dividing the total moment by the total weight gives the Center of Gravity position:

$$\frac{218,650}{2,382} = 91.79 \text{ inches aft of datum}$$

When the weight and CG position is plotted on the graph, it shows that the aircraft is loaded to fall within the NORMAL category. However, you can see that we are only allowing for some fairly light people and little baggage. You are unlikely to be able to fill a Cherokee with four adults, full fuel and full baggage and still be within limits. It is up to the pilot-in-command to decide what to leave on the ground!

A WORD OF WARNING. As well as the safety aspect, operating the aircraft outside its weight and balance envelope has far reaching legal and financial implications. Almost the first thing an accident investigator will check after an accident is the loading of the aircraft. If the loading is outside limits the pilot is violating the Federal Aviation Regulations. In addition, both the aircraft insurance company and your personal insurance company will be unsympathetic when they know that the conditions of the Airworthiness Certificate (i.e., the flight manual limitations) were not complied with. As the pilot-in-command the responsibility is yours alone. The fact that the aircraft has four seats does not necessarily mean that the aircraft can be flown with all four seats occupied, baggage and full fuel load.

PA-28-180 Cherokee Weight vs. Center of Gravity

PA-28-140 Cherokee Weight vs. Center of Gravity

Performance

The Cherokee flight manual contains a section of graphs to allow the pilot to calculate the expected performance of the aircraft for different flight phases. The most commonly used graphs are those for takeoff and landing performance, and those are the ones we will concentrate on here. However, the same principles can be used on the other graphs. Two things to remember: First, the chart performance is obtained by using the recommended techniques—to get graph results follow graph procedures. Second, you can safely assume that the graph results have been obtained by placing a brand new aircraft in the hands of an experienced test pilot under favorable conditions. To make allowances for a less than new aircraft, being flown by an average mortal in real conditions, it is wise to "factor" any results you get. As with loading calculations, the pilot must use the graphs and data from the documents for the individual aircraft being used. The graphs and diagrams used in this section are for illustrative purposes only, and not for operational use.

In Section 7, conversion factors between feet and meters are listed, together with recommended factors for variations not necessarily covered by the flight manual graphs.

PA-28 Cherokee Takeoff and Landing Performance Graphs

The takeoff distance and landing distance graphs in the flight manual make several assumptions: paved, dry, runway, use of flight manual technique.

The graphs use the term "Pressure Altitude." This is the altitude of the runway assuming a standard pressure setting (i.e., 29.92" Hg). On a day with a pressure other than 29.92 you will need to adjust the actual altitude to get the pressure altitude. For instance, on a day with a pressure above 29.92 the pressure altitude will be less than the actual, and vice versa. To do this conversion, simply adjust the actual altitude by 1,000 feet for each inch Hg above or below 29.92" (10 feet for each .01").

The headwind or tailwind component is calculated from the wind speed and the angle to the runway (i.e., a 10 knot wind directly down the runway gives a headwind component of 10 knots. A 10 knot wind at 90° to the runway gives a headwind component of 0). There is a graph in Section 7 for calculating head/tail wind component and crosswind component.

The takeoff distance and landing distance graphs will state the technique used to obtain the figures. Remember, to get graph results you have to use the graph techniques.

Takeoff Performance

The takeoff performance can be divided into two sections:

The Takeoff Run (or Takeoff Ground Roll), the distance taken for the aircraft to become airborne, and;

The Takeoff Distance, that is the total distance required for the aircraft to become airborne *and* clear a 50' barrier.

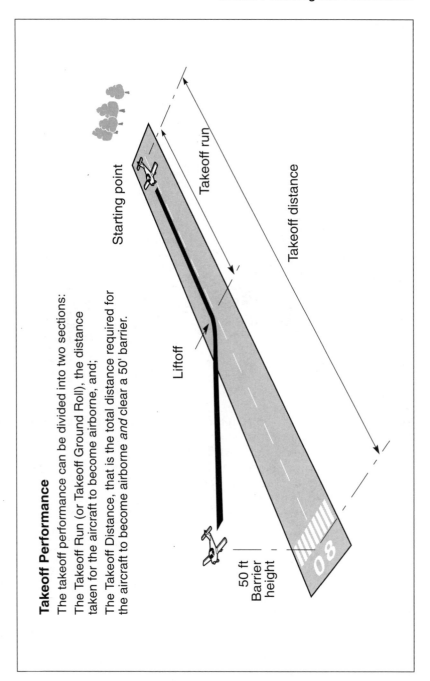

Starting point

Takeoff run

Takeoff distance

Liftoff

50 ft
Barrier
height

0 8

Takeoff Distance Calculation Example

For this example we will take the conditions as:

Outside Air Temperature +25°C
Pressure Altitude 1,500 feet
Takeoff weight 1,700 lbs
Headwind Component 10 Knots

Start at the temperature (+25°C) go vertically to the pressure altitude of 1,500 feet, and then go horizontally to the REFERENCE LINE. From this point, parallel the guideline until above the 1,700 lbs point. From this point take a line horizontally to the next reference line and then follow the guide line until above the 10 knots point. From this point take a line horizontally to the far side of the graph and read the takeoff distance of 2,200 feet.

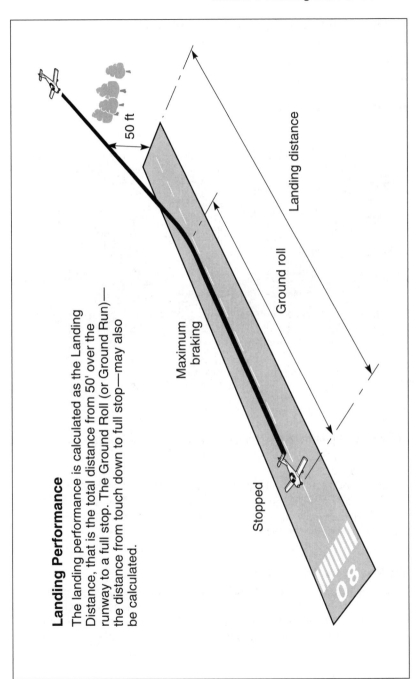

Landing Performance

The landing performance is calculated as the Landing Distance, that is the total distance from 50' over the runway to a full stop. The Ground Roll (or Ground Run)—the distance from touch down to full stop—may also be calculated.

Landing Distance Calculation Example

For this example we will take the conditions as:

Outside Air Temperature +20°C
Pressure Altitude Sea Level
Landing weight 1,700 lbs
Headwind Component 10 knots

On the landing distance graph, start at the temperature (+20°C) and go vertically to the Sea Level line. From this point go horizontally to the REFERENCE LINE, and then along the guideline until above the 1,700 lbs point. Then go horizontally to the wind reference line. From the reference line, parallel the headwind guidelines until above the 10 knots point. From here take the line horizontally to the far side of the graph and read the landing distance in feet—1,150 feet.

En Route Performance

Data may also be provided in the flight manual for calculating the en route performance, such as climb performance. These graphs are tackled using the same technique as for the takeoff and landing graphs. Remember, to get graph results, use the graph techniques.

PA-28-140 Cherokee Takeoff Distance
Paved Level Dry Runway, Flaps 25°

PA-28-140 Cherokee Landing Distance
Paved Level Dry Runway, Flaps 40°

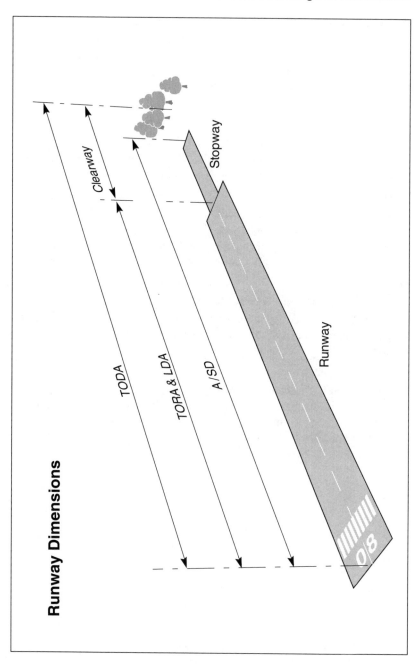

Runway Dimensions

Runway Dimensions

Having calculated the distances the aircraft requires for takeoff or landing, the runway dimensions must be checked to ensure that the aircraft can be safely operated on the runway in question. The figures given in the Airport/Facility Directory or airfield guide can be defined in a number of ways.

The Takeoff Run Available (TORA)

The TORA is the length of the runway available for the takeoff ground run of the aircraft. This is usually the physical length of the runway.

Accelerate/Stop Distance (A/SD)

The A/SD is the length of the TORA plus the length of any stopway. A stopway is the area at the end of the TORA prepared for an aircraft to stop on in the event of an abandoned takeoff.

The Takeoff Distance Available (TODA)

The TODA is the TORA plus the length of any clearway. A clearway is an area over which an aircraft may make its initial climb (to 50' in this instance).

The Landing Distance Available (LDA)

The LDA is the length of the runway available for the ground run of an aircraft landing. In all cases the landing distance required should never be greater than the landing distance available.

PA-28-140
Cherokee

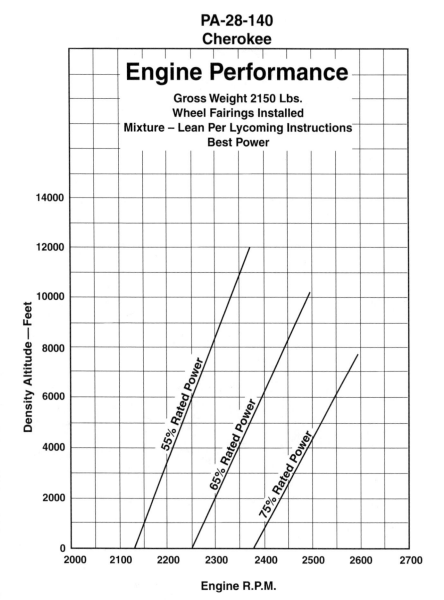

Engine Performance

Gross Weight 2150 Lbs.
Wheel Fairings Installed
Mixture – Lean Per Lycoming Instructions
Best Power

Engine R.P.M.

Note: See Section 7 of the Pilot's Operating Handbook for
Effects of Air Conditioning Installation on Performance.

PA-28-140
Cherokee

Cruise Performance – True Airspeed

Gross Weight 2150 Lbs.
No Wheel Fairings Installed
Mixture – Lean Per Lycoming Instructions
Best Power

Full Throttle

Note: Add 3 MPH when wheel fairings are installed.

55% Rated Power
65% Rated Power
75% Rated Power

Density Altitude — Feet

True Airspeed—M.P.H.

Note: See Section 7 of the Pilot's Operating Handbook for
Effects of Air Conditioning Installation on Performance.

PA-28-140
Cherokee

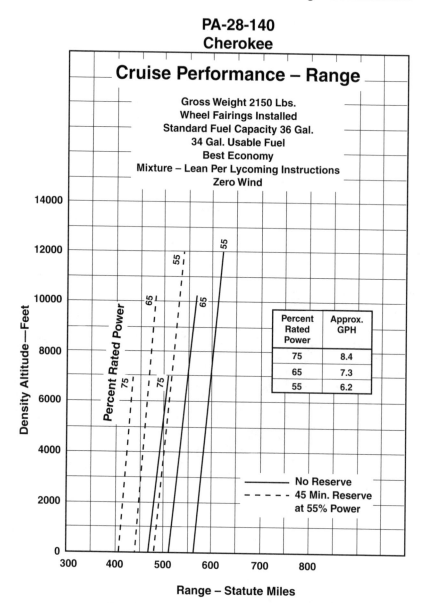

Cruise Performance – Range

Gross Weight 2150 Lbs.
Wheel Fairings Installed
Standard Fuel Capacity 36 Gal.
34 Gal. Usable Fuel
Best Economy
Mixture – Lean Per Lycoming Instructions
Zero Wind

Percent Rated Power	Approx. GPH
75	8.4
65	7.3
55	6.2

—————— No Reserve
- - - - - 45 Min. Reserve at 55% Power

Density Altitude—Feet (vertical axis: 0, 2000, 4000, 6000, 8000, 10000, 12000, 14000)

Range – Statute Miles (horizontal axis: 300, 400, 500, 600, 700, 800)

Note: See Section 7 of the Pilot's Operating Handbook for
Effects of Air Conditioning Installation on Performance.

Section 7
Conversions

PA-28 Cherokee A Pilot's Guide

Takeoff Distance Factors

The following factors will allow the pilot to make allowance for variations that may affect takeoff performance. Although some of these factors are covered in the Cherokee performance tables, the table is produced in its entirety for completeness:

VARIATION	INCREASE IN TAKEOFF DISTANCE (to 50')	FACTOR
10% increase in aircraft weight	20%	1.2
Increase of 1,000' in runway altitude	10%	1.1
Increase in temperature of 10°C	10%	1.1
Dry Grass		
—Short (under 5 inches)	20%	1.2
—Long (5 – 10 inches)	25%	1.25
Wet Grass		
—Short	25%	1.25
—Long	30%	1.3
2% uphill slope	10%	1.1
Tailwind component of 10% of lift-off speed	20%	1.2
Soft ground or snow *	at least 25%	at least 1.25

* snow and other runway contamination are covered on page 7-5.

Landing Distance Factors

The following factors will allow the pilot to make allowance for variations that may affect landing performance. Although some of these factors are covered in the Cherokee performance tables, the table is produced in its entirety for completeness:

VARIATION	INCREASE IN LANDING DISTANCE (from 50')	FACTOR
10% increase in aircraft weight	10%	1.1
Increase of 1,000' in runway altitude	5%	1.05
Increase in temperature of 10°C	5%	1.05
Dry Grass		
—Short (under 5 inches)	20%	1.2
—Long (5 – 10 inches)	30%	1.3
Wet Grass		
—Short	30%	1.3
—Long	40%	1.4
2% downhill slope	10%	1.1
Tailwind component of 10% of landing speed	20%	1.2
snow *	at least 25%	at least 1.25

* snow and other runway contamination are covered on page 7-5.

Runway Contamination

A runway can be contaminated by water, snow or slush. If operation on such a runway cannot be avoided additional allowance must be made for the problems such contamination may cause—i.e., additional drag, reduced braking performance (possible hydroplaning), and directional control problems.

It is generally recommended that takeoff should not be attempted if dry snow covers the runway to a depth of more than 2", or if water, slush or wet snow covers the runway to more than 1/2". In addition, a tailwind, or crosswind component exceeding 10 knots, should not be accepted when operating on a slippery runway.

For takeoff distance required calculations, the other known conditions should be factored, and the accelerate/stop distance available on the runway should be at least 2.0 x the takeoff distance required (for a paved runway) or at least 2.66 x the takeoff distance required (for a grass runway).

Any water or slush can have a very adverse effect on landing performance, and the danger of hydroplaning (with negligible wheel braking and loss of directional control) is very real.

Use of the Wind Component Graph

This graph can be used to find the head/tail wind component and the crosswind component, given a particular wind velocity and runway direction.

EXAMPLE:

Runway 27

Surface wind 240°/15 knots

The angle between the runway direction (270°) and wind direction(240°) is 30°. Now on the graph locate a point on the 30° line, where it crosses the 15 knot arc. From this point take a horizontal line to give the headwind component (13 knots) and a vertical line to give the crosswind component (8 knots).

On the main graph overleaf the shaded area represents the maximum demonstrated crosswind component for this aircraft. If the wind point is within this shaded area, the maximum demonstrated cross-wind component for this aircraft has been exceeded.

Note:
Runway direction will be degrees magnetic. Check the wind direction given is also in degrees magnetic.

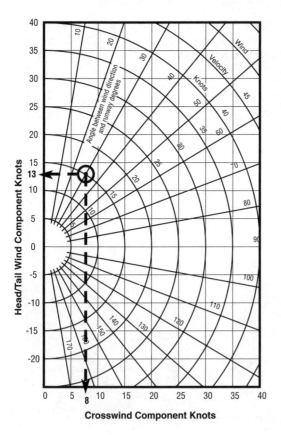

Crosswind Component Knots

Wind Component Graph

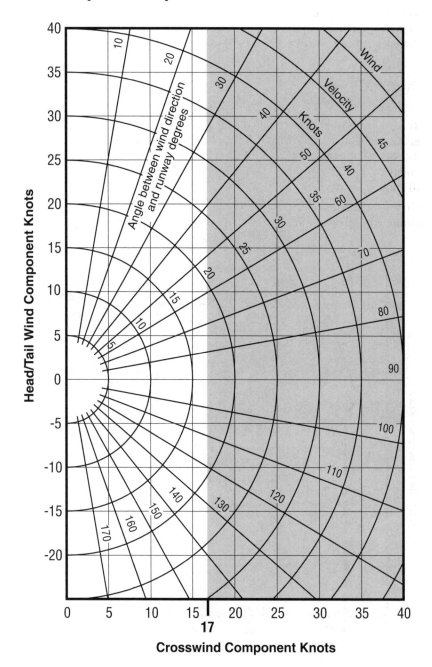

Crosswind Component Knots

Temperature

Distance – Meters/Feet

Meters	Feet	Feet	Meters
1	3.28	1	0.30
2	6.56	2	0.61
3	9.84	3	0.91
4	13.12	4	1.22
5	16.40	5	1.52
6	19.69	6	1.83
7	22.97	7	2.13
8	26.25	8	2.44
9	29.53	9	2.74
10	32.81	10	3.05
20	65.62	20	6.10
30	98.43	30	9.14
40	131.23	40	12.19
50	164.04	50	15.24
60	196.85	60	18.29
70	229.66	70	21.34
80	262.47	80	24.38
90	295.28	90	27.43
100	328.08	100	30.48
200	656.16	200	60.96
300	984.25	300	91.44
400	1,312.34	400	121.92
500	1,640.42	500	152.40
600	1,968.50	600	182.88
700	2,296.59	700	213.36
800	2,624.67	800	243.84
900	2,952.76	900	274.32
1,000	3,280.84	1,000	304.80
2,000	6,561.70	2,000	609.60
3,000	9,842.50	3,000	914.40
4,000	13,123.40	4,000	1,219.20
5,000	16,404.20	5,000	1,524.00
6,000	19,685.00	6,000	1,828.80
7,000	22,965.90	7,000	2,133.60
8,000	26,246.70	8,000	2,438.40
9,000	29,527.60	9,000	2,743.20
10,000	32,808.40	10,000	3,048.00

Conversion Factors:

Centimeters to Inches x .3937　　Meters to Feet x 3.28084
Inches to Centimeters x 2.54　　Feet to Meters x 0.3048

Distance – Nautical Miles / Statute Miles

NM	SM		SM	NM
1	1.15		1	.87
2	2.30		2	1.74
3	3.45		3	2.61
4	4.60		4	3.48
5	5.75		5	4.34
6	6.90		6	5.21
7	8.06		7	6.08
8	9.21		8	6.95
9	10.36		9	7.82
10	11.51		10	8.69
20	23.02		20	17.38
30	34.52		30	26.07
40	46.03		40	34.76
50	57.54		50	43.45
60	69.05		60	52.14
70	80.55		70	60.83
80	92.06		80	69.52
90	103.57		90	78.21
100	115.1		100	86.9
200	230.2		200	173.8
300	345.2		300	260.7
400	460.3		400	347.6
500	575.4		500	434.5
600	690.5		600	521.4
700	805.6		700	608.3
800	920.6		800	695.2
900	1035.7		900	782.1

Conversion Factors:

Statute Miles to Nautical Miles x 0.868976
Nautical Miles to Statute Miles x 1.15078

Volume (Fluid)

Liters	U.S. Gal.		U.S. Gal.	Liters
1	0.26		1	3.79
2	0.53		2	7.57
3	0.79		3	11.36
4	1.06		4	15.14
5	1.32		5	18.93
6	1.59		6	22.71
7	1.85		7	26.50
8	2.11		8	30.28
9	2.38		9	34.07
10	2.64		10	37.85
20	5.28		20	75.71
30	7.93		30	113.56
40	10.57		40	151.41
50	13.21		50	189.27
60	15.85		60	227.12
70	18.49		70	264.97
80	21.14		80	302.82
90	23.78		90	340.68
100	26.42		100	378.54
200	52.84			
300	79.26			
400	105.68			
500	132.10			
600	158.52			
700	184.94			
800	211.36			
900	237.78			
1000	264.20			

Conversion Factors:

U.S. Gallons to Liters x 3.78541
Liters to U.S. Gallons x 0.264179

PA-28 Cherokee Index